Key to the Wine Cellar

Savoring the Word With the Rosary

By Sister Mary Rose Reddy, DMML

Copyright: Daughters of Mary, Mother of Healing Love, 2015; Rochester, NH, U.S.A.

ISBN- 978-1-940128-23-8

Cover photo: Sunrise on the Atlantic Ocean taken by Mother Paul Marie on July 5, 2010. Rosary beads were made from roses from Adam Keenan's funeral.

Table of Contents

Dedication 7

Acknowledgements 8

Recommendation by Most Reverend Peter A. Libasci, D.D., Bishop of Manchester 10

Introduction: Entering Most Deeply into the Spirit through the Body 12

Chapter One: --My Story of Conversion through the Rosary 14

Chapter Two: The Gift of the Rosary--A History of the Rosary 19

Chapter Three: Partakers of a Heavenly Calling--Praying the Rosary 25

Words of the Rosary prayers: 28

Quick View of How to Pray the Rosary 29

How to Pray the Rosary Using This Book 31

Chapter Four: Cause of Our Joy--The Joyful Mysteries 32

Chapter Five: Doorway to the Depths of the Heart of Christ--Luminous Mysteries 44

Chapter Six: The Immeasurable Riches of His Grace--The Sorrowful Mysteries 58

Chapter Seven: Clothed with Power from on High--The Glorious Mysteries 72

Chapter Eight: At the Hour of Our Death—Intercessory Power of the Rosary 84

The Story of Adam Keenan 84

Conclusion 90

Endnotes 92

Bibliography 94

Photography credits: 96

Fifteen Promises of the Rosary 97

About the Author's Religious Community: 101

Lifeline Against Suicide Team (L.A.S.T.) Prayer 101

O God, who by the glorification of your Christ

And the light of the Holy Spirit

Have unlocked for us the gates of eternity,

Grant, we pray,

That, partaking of so great a gift,

Our devotion may grow deeper

And our faith be strengthened.

Through our Lord Jesus Christ, your Son,

Who lives and reigns with you in the unity of the Holy Spirit,

One God, for ever and ever.

(Collect for Friday of the Seventh week of Easter)

Am I not here who am your Mother? Are you not under my shadow and protection?
Am I not your fountain of life? Are you not in the folds of my mantle?
In the crossing of my arms? Is there anything else you need?"

(Our Lady to St. Juan Diego, Dec. 1531).

Dedication

It is my conviction that women not only hand on physical life, but also hand on spiritual life. With this in mind I dedicate this book to eight women who have been very influential in handing on life to me. First, I dedicate it to my own mother who loved the Rosary. As she was near death in December 2009, I asked her to tell God when she got up to Heaven that I wanted to write a book. She agreed to do this. Six weeks after she died I received the invitation to write the six articles for *Parable Magazine* on which this book is based.

I dedicate it to my "second mother," my Aunt Mame, who gave me the gift of the Rosary when I most needed it. She also loved the Rosary; she prayed it every day and she made hundreds of rosaries for the missions.

I dedicate it to Mother Paul Marie, my spiritual mother, and the foundress of the Daughters of Mary, Mother of Healing Love, who has helped me greatly with her wisdom and insight.

I dedicate it to Sarah Jane Lavery, another of my spiritual mothers, whose recommendation led to my writing the magazine articles on which this book is based.

I dedicate it to my sister, Kate Reddy, whose loving personality is a continual source of new life to me and whose great gift for uniting friends and keeping them together brings joyful new life to many.

I dedicate it to Mother M. Bernard, SCMC, my prayer partner for many years, whose love and prayers have been such a great gift to me.

I dedicate it to St. Anne, the mother of Mary and the grandmother of Jesus who directly influenced my decision to become a Sister.

And lastly, I dedicate it to Mary, Mother of Healing Love, who used the Rosary to draw me out of the pits of despair into the joy that no one can take away. May she use this book to open the door for you to taste the eternal joy that God has prepared for you from all eternity.

Ed and Char Reddy

Acknowledgements

I am grateful to God for His Infinite Mercy in calling us back to Himself and in giving us the gift of Mary, our Mother of Healing Love, and her holy Rosary. Just as the Rosary is made up of many links, there are very many people who have contributed in one way or another to this book's completion. Although they are too many to list by name, I thank them all. In particular, though, I want to thank: Sarah Jane von Haack, the editor of *Parable Magazine*, for providing advice and insight, Larry Landolfi, professional photographer, for his invaluable advice regarding the illustrations, and Marcia Young (d. 2013) for her editing assistance. I also owe a particular thanks to Jeanne Degen who provided me with irreplaceable help in getting this book published.

I thank Mother Paul Marie and the Daughters of Mary, Mother of Healing Love and my family (especially Vince, Kath, Doug, Uncle John, Mick, Linda, Jid, Wendy), and friends (especially Gloria Anson, Susan Bellavance, Jude Christopher, Andrea Harris, Judith Hughes, Karla LaRochelle, Sarah Jane Lavery, Bob and Brenda Lloyd, Jackie Pelletier, Marty Rotella, Kathy Towne, Lynne and Sam Ventura, Meg Wood) for all their love, prayers, help, and encouragement. I especially thank Mother Paul Marie for her help with the photography and Sister Esther Marie for her help with the setup of the book. I am indebted to Father John Hardon, S.J. (d. 2000) for my clarity of understanding the faith and my love for memorizing Scripture. I am indebted to my own father, Edward Reddy (d. 2008), and to my aunt, Sister Mary Robert, CSJ (d. 1993) for their influence on me as a writer. I thank Christopher West for his inspired teaching.

I am indebted to the Keenan family for their beautiful witness of faith and love. I'm grateful to Mother Marie Alma (d. 1995), Mother M. Bernard, Sister John Baptist (d. 2011), and the Sisters of Charity of Our Lady, Mother of the Church. I appreciate the many priests who have helped me, especially, Father Bill Gaffney, C.Ss.R., Father Paul Gousse, Father Ray Introvigne, and Father Michael Taylor. I am especially grateful to Bishop Peter A. Libasci, Bishop of Manchester, NH, for taking the time out of his busy schedule to read the book and to support and encourage its publication.

Lastly I acknowledge my Guardian Angel who continues to do an excellent job with a difficult assignment!

OFFICE OF THE BISHOP
DIOCESE OF MANCHESTER

Bishop Peter Libasci's Recommendation

After reading Sister's book it dawned on me that the powerful prayer of the Rosary never becomes tired, is never out of date-- but by the Wisdom of our Blessed Lady remains a refreshing and renewing oasis of prayer. In *the Key to the Wine Cellar* Sister does enable us to savor the Word of God as it is recalled anew each time we pray the Rosary. Chapter by chapter Sister draws us in to reread and to remember the Mysteries of our salvation that are renewed in each lifetime.

I encourage you, dear reader, to go as I did to savor again the Mysteries. If you are in the habit of praying the Rosary and even have done so for many, many years, this wonderful little work is not without its surprises and insights. And if indeed you love the Rosary, this book will help you to introduce it to those for whom it is an unknown treasure. Sister's words and style are approachable and engaging so that one for whom the Rosary is a new discovery will easily be drawn into its fragrance, its simplicity, and its rich depth of meaning.

At the conclusion of this book is the story of the Rosary's powerful influence in the lives of the Keenan family at the time of the sudden death of their son, Adam. I met Adam's parents and his sister, Christine and I spoke with them. I was profoundly impressed that through the faith of this family, and through the mysterious influence of the Rosary, what could have been just a dark tragedy was instead transformed into the mysterious darkness of a wine cellar—holding in its recesses the promise of exhilarating joy and eternal reunion.

+ *[signature]*

Most Reverend Peter A. Libasci, D.D.
Bishop of Manchester
June 27, 2014
Solemnity of the Most Sacred Heart of Jesus

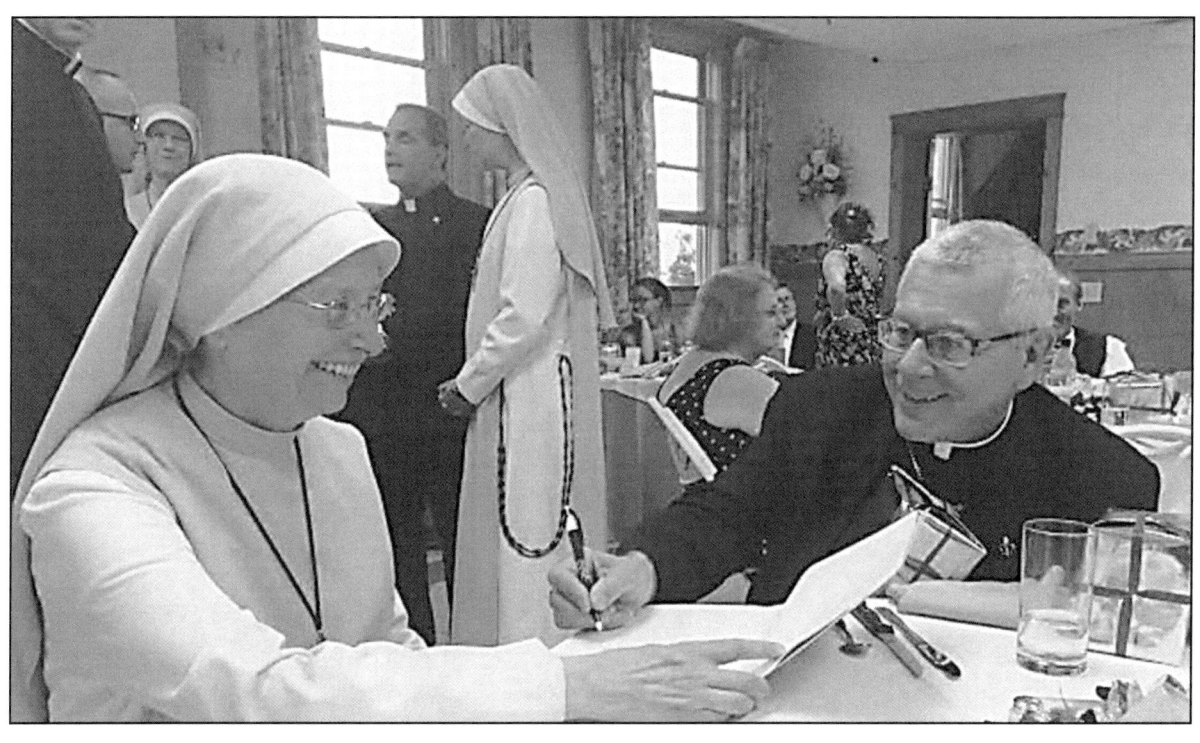

Most Reverend Peter A. Libasci, D.D. Bishop of Manchester signing his recommendation of _Key to the Wine Cellar_ for Sister Mary Rose on June 27, 2014

Introduction:
Entering Most Deeply into the Spirit through the Body

"He brought me into the cellar of wine;
He set in order charity in me" (Song of Songs 2:4).

Everyone is looking for the perfect love, but not everyone knows that the Perfect Love is looking for each of us.

Some people focus their attention on sexual attraction; others try to ignore sexual attraction and focus on spirituality. Neither of these makes sense. We will find the Perfect Love when we allow Him to integrate our sexuality and our spirituality because we are embodied persons and can't live happily split in half. Christopher West says that we find **the key to the wine cellar** when we realize that the loving sexual union of husband and wife in marriage is the true icon of the loving Eucharistic union of Christ with His Bride, the Church (West, pg. 74). Meditating on the mysteries of the Rosary is one of the ways to open the door to the transforming power of this "great mystery" (cf. Ephesians 5:31-32).

Knowing our identity as Bride enables us to be fruitful. Just as the sexual union of husband and wife opens the door to life, the sacramental union of Christ with His Bride opens the door to the Spirit, the Lord and giver of Life.

There are unfathomable depths to the Spirit, but the Rosary draws us ever deeper into Him; because it is the Mercy of God that we absorb in the Rosary. Jesus said to Saint Faustina, "Today bring to me the souls who especially venerate and glorify My mercy, and immerse them in My mercy. These souls sorrowed most over My Passion **and entered most deeply into My Spirit**" (Diary, 1224).

Take this key, then, and enter into the wine cellar of Divine Love. *Remember who you became through your Baptism.* Remember that despite the sad circumstances surrounding you, the completion of your earthly mission and your entrance into the full and eternal communion of saints is being awaited with joyful anticipation.

The Lost Key

Once not long after I learned to drive, I found myself in the embarrassing situation of having locked myself out of the car while it was still running in the middle of the road. I was right out in front of Sacred Heart Church, so I went in to call my father to ask him to bring me another key.

The key for interpreting reality, according to Saint John Paul II, is that original sin attempts to abolish Fatherhood.[1] Before original sin, Adam and Eve knew the Father and walked with Him in the garden. It is the desire of Our Heavenly Father that we would leave sin behind and regain this intimacy and the experience of His loving presence in our innermost being.

Meditating with Our Lady on the mysteries of the Holy Rosary opens the Heart of the Word of God to us. In the Sacred Heart of Jesus the fullness of the Holy Spirit abides. Abiding in the Word, we learn to call, "Abba, Father!" Call Our Father. Tell Him you're calling from Sacred Heart, and you can't move forward till He brings you another key.

Chapter One: --My Story of Conversion through the Rosary

"And no one pours new wine into old wineskins; else the new wine will burst the skins, and will be spilt itself, and the skins ruined. But new wine must be put into fresh skins, and both are saved"
(Luke 5:37, 38).

In 1979, when I dropped out of college for the second time, praying the Rosary was the farthest thought from my mind. In fact, I was out of my mind. Months of drinking, taking various drugs, and reading the depressive literature of my college curriculum, had finally brought me to a point of insanity where I was certain that all reality was subjective and that it was my responsibility to die to end the chaos. Resolving not to eat or drink again, I arrived at my aunt and uncle's home in Exton, Pennsylvania, with the intention of leaving by train the next morning to find a way to end my life.

Then it began to snow. Exton is not a place that typically gets much snow. (We Syracuse, New York, natives used to make fun of Exton's overreaction to even a few inches!) But that night it snowed so much that I couldn't leave in the morning. I remember being angry about this and being so thirsty that I wanted to eat the snow.

Suddenly my Aunt Mame came into the room. She gave me a blue plastic Rosary and a scapular of Our Lady of Mount Carmel (a brown scapular) and then she turned around and left. I hadn't prayed in a very long time, but I decided to put on the brown scapular and then I began to pray the Rosary.

Immediately, light began to fill my mind. I came back to reality and I saw the terrible state of my soul. I prayed another Rosary and I thought for a long time about my life. I could see how God had given me so many blessings and opportunities that I'd thrown away- such as the scholarships I'd had when I graduated from high school. I could see the graces that He'd given me by allowing me to born into a Catholic family, to receive the Sacraments, and to attend a Catholic school. I could see how gifted I was to have a father, mother, sister, and brother who loved me. It was as if God allowed me to review my whole life and consider all the gifts that I had taken for granted and wasted.

The next day, instead of leaving to end my life, I left to go into Philadelphia to Saint Bridget's Church for Confession. After I had confessed all the sins that I could remember, the priest said to me, "You could become a saint you know." This shocked me and almost made me wonder if he was deaf.

Then began the most difficult and painful year of my life in which I struggled to believe that God had forgiven me for my sins and in which I felt as if I were damned. I thought that because in my insanity I had believed that reality was subjective, that this had been a sin against the Holy Spirit. Priests and others tried to explain to me why this was wrong thinking, but it seemed like they were just saying these things to make me feel better and my heart was not convinced.

People who have not gone through this experience cannot understand what an extreme depth of anguish the thought that one is damned can bring a person to. It seems to me that all the subsequent sufferings of my life have been minor compared to the interior pain I experienced at that time. Bishop Fulton Sheen said that when Jesus cried out to his Father as he was dying, "My God, my God, why have you forsaken me?" (Matthew 27:46) it was to redeem those who were experiencing this unbearable thought that their souls had been lost forever.

During these agonizing months it was Our Lady who through the brown scapular and the Rosary kept me clinging to the hope of salvation. I never would take off the brown scapular during that year because of the promise that Our Lady had given to Saint Simon Stock in 1251: "Whoever dies clothed in this scapular will not suffer eternal fire."[2]

I wish that I could say that after I had gone to Confession at Saint Bridget's I always remained in the state of grace but this was not the case. In fact, during that year I sometimes veered back into drinking, drugs, and immoral relationships; but I found that what used to be fun for me had become extremely depressing.

One December night as I was returning from a bar, I was riding my bike past a cemetery when suddenly I was hit from behind by a car. At the moment of impact I remember thinking, "I could die," but then I was thrown off my bike. Although my bike was smashed beyond repair, I had only a bruise on my leg and I knew with great clarity that Our Lady, through the brown scapular, which is her mantle, had saved me from death. I also knew that any good that would ever come out of my life would be thanks to her intervention at that moment.

After this fall and all the other falls, I would again go to Confession and then I would go to the opposite extreme: always praying, being in Church, fasting, and trying to do good things. I became extremely scrupulous and tried to buy God's favor by doing every good thing that I could think of to do. I really didn't know God then, and I was trying to buy my way back into His favor. Obviously this didn't work because God doesn't love us because of what we do or don't do, but because of who we are — unique reflections of His infinite Beauty.

During all these months I always kept praying the Rosary and since I had alienated all of the friends I had grown up with (due to my fanaticism), Our Lady sent other people into my life to help me. One of them was a 79 year old woman from Ireland named Mary Ann Frances Ryan. She was a beggar whom I met one day in downtown Syracuse. She understood my soul and she was sometimes able to influence me to pray rather than to fall back into sin. Later on, after I was healed, and I told her that I was going to enter the convent, she worried how she would get along without my help (I used to bring her food.) but she died a happy death on August 5, 1980 — just 11 days before I entered the convent.

Another person who helped me was one of my mother's friends who gave me a copy of *True Devotion to Mary* by Saint. Louis de Montfort. I read this book and did the 33 days of preparation to consecrate myself to Jesus through Mary. When the day came for me to make the consecration, March 25, 1980, I was in Philadelphia visiting one of my friends and so I was able to make this consecration in the Shrine of Our Lady of the Miraculous Medal in Germantown, Pennsylvania. Making this consecration was a major turning point in my life. From the moment I made this consecration, the feeling that I was damned left me, and it has never returned.

Our Lady took very seriously the consecration I had made to her in which I had turned my whole life including all the good and all the bad over to her. In some way I no longer was just living in myself but I knew that I was living in her Immaculate Heart. From within her heart I finally had the capacity for the "new wine" that God had been desiring to give me for such a long time. I understood on a personal level what it means that Our Lady is the Immaculate Conception because in her I knew that God was allowing me to make a clean start. I would not be lost forever. I could learn to know and love Jesus, the Holy Spirit, and the Father.

Praying the Rosary every day came to be as important to me as eating. I no longer worried about falling back into sin because I knew that I could rely on Our Lady's help to stay in the state of grace. Another change was that I began to know God personally; it made me joyful to do the right thing and I wasn't just doing the right thing to try to "earn" God's favor.

It was then that the desire of my young childhood to become a Sister came back to me. I knew, though, that I would have to be a Sister in full habit and that I would have to find a place where I could live the consecrated life in its fullness. This was because I knew that in lay clothes and without a structured religious life I would probably become very worldly again. But I didn't know any Sisters in full habit in central New York. On June 18, 1980, I was in New York City and I saw a Sister wearing a habit; I asked her if she knew of any orders that wore the full habit. She gave me the address of the Sisters of Charity of Our Lady, Mother of the Church in Connecticut. That same night, the mother of one of those Sisters gave me the same address.

I wrote to the Sisters of Charity and Mother Marie Alma, who was the superior general at the time, called me and invited me to come to visit. I tried to put her off, saying that I had no money, but she was very insistent and so on July 2, 1980, I went to visit the Sisters in Baltic, Connecticut. The first day I really liked being there, but then the second day I suddenly started thinking, "What am I doing here with all of these holy Sisters?" and I wanted to bolt out of the room. But then one of the Sisters, who later became my friend, prayed for me and this temptation went away.

After I returned to Syracuse I wanted to join the Sisters of Charity but I still was uncertain if this was God's will. I felt that since I had sinned so much, He might not want me to become a Sister. And so I made a pilgrimage to the Shrine of Saint Anne de Beaupre (the mother of the Blessed Mother) in Quebec to ask God if He wanted me to become a Sister. On July 25, 1980, there was a candlelight Rosary procession at the shrine. After the procession the priest invited anyone who wanted to venerate the relic of Saint Anne to come forward. (This relic is a chip of bone from her arm enclosed in a small reliquary.[3]) As each person kissed the relic the priest would say, "Saint Anne, bless you," but when I kissed the relic the priest (whom I had never met) said, "Saint Anne, bless you. And make you a nun, by the way."

On August 16, 1980, I joined the Sisters of Charity of Our Lady, Mother of the Church in Baltic, Connecticut. I was a Sister of Charity until September 19, 2003 when a small group of us formed a new Association of Sisters called the Daughters of Mary, Mother of Healing Love to work specifically for the healing of children and families.

The joy that filled my soul at the moment when the priest said, "And make you a nun, by the way," is a joy that no set of circumstances since then has ever been able to take away. It was Our Lady who through the Rosary led me to that joy and it is with everlasting gratitude to her for my own life and vocation that I desire to give you this **key to the wine cellar.**

Chapter Two: The Gift of the Rosary--A History of the Rosary

The Rosary is a gift from the Mother of God to each of us. In the year 1214, Saint Dominic spent three days in a forest near Toulouse, France, praying fervently to Our Lady that she would show him how he could bring people back to God, especially those who were adhering to the Albigensian heresy, which denied the goodness of the body. Our Lady appeared to Saint Dominic and told him that the Angelic Psalter (the Hail Mary) was the foundation stone of the New Testament and that he should preach the Rosary. Saint Dominic and his followers found the Rosary to be a very effective means of leading people into the kingdom of heaven.[4]

Jesus said, "The kingdom of heaven is like a treasure hidden in a field; he who finds it hides it, and in his joy goes and sells all he has and buys that field." (Matthew 13:44) In the field of Our Lady's Rosary we find the treasure of the Incarnate Word. In the Rosary 58% of the words come directly from Sacred Scripture while another 16% come directly from Sacred Tradition. Of the remaining words, 5% were taught by Our Lady at Fatima in 1917 and the other 21% come from popular piety going back many centuries.

Saint John Paul II highly recommended reading Scripture along with praying the Rosary.[5] As the following table illustrates, in the Gospels alone there are more than 600 verses which refer directly to one of the 20 Rosary mysteries:

Table 1

Joyful Mysteries	Matthew	Mark	Luke	John
Annunciation	1:18-25		1:26-38	
Visitation			1:39-56	
Nativity	2:1-11		2:1-20	1:14
Presentation			2:22-39	
Finding of the Child Jesus in the Temple			2:41-52	

Table 2

Luminous Mysteries	Matthew	Mark	Luke	John
Baptism of Jesus	3:13-17	1:9-11	3:21-22	1:29-34
Wedding Feast at Cana				2:1-12
Proclamation of the Kingdom	10:1-42	1:15; 2:3-13	7:47-48; 9:1-6	18:33-37
Transfiguration	17:1-13	9:1-12	9:28-36	1:14
Institution of the Eucharist	26:26-29	14:22-25	22:14-20	6:22-70; 13:1

Table 3

Sorrowful Mysteries	Matthew	Mark	Luke	John
Agony in the Garden	26:36-55	14:32-52	22:39-53	18:1-11
Scourging at the Pillar	27:26	15:15	18:32-33	19:1
Crowning with Thorns	27:29	15:18		19:2
Carrying of the Cross	27:31-32	15:20-22	23:26-32	19:17
Crucifixion	27:35-50	15:24-41	23:33-49	19:18-30

Table 4

Glorious Mysteries	Matthew	Mark	Luke	John
Resurrection of Jesus	28:1-20	16:1-18	24:1-49	20:1-31; 21:1-23
Ascension of Jesus		16:19-20	24:50-52	3:13; 6:62-63
Descent of the Holy Spirit			24:49	14:16-17; 15:26;
Assumption of Mary			1:49, 52	
Crowning of Mary Queen of Heaven and Earth			1:48-49	

In the prayer of the Rosary as we greet Mary over and over with the word, "Hail," our hearts experience the effects of her return greeting; these are to be filled with the Holy Spirit and with joy and to recognize the presence of Jesus within her. "When Elizabeth heard the greeting of Mary, the babe in her womb leapt. And Elizabeth was filled with the Holy Spirit and cried out with a loud voice, saying, 'Blessed art thou among women and blessed is the fruit of thy womb!'" (Luke 1:41-44)

Meditation on the mysteries is essential to the Rosary, but it is the repetition of the same words over and over that provides an intellectual space where we encounter the Word of God. This is because there is an element of our thinking that can never be stilled even when we are asleep, but the repetition of the same words serves to still this restlessness while opening a kind of silence in the soul. In that silence the Word of God enters. We become aware of being in His presence and in the presence of Our Lady. We then communicate our concerns and receive the healing power of the words of God to help us to deal with particular situations. Saint John Paul II once wrote, "To pray the Rosary is to hand over our burdens to the merciful hearts of Christ and his Mother."[6]

Some people find the Rosary to be boring and repetitious and very difficult to pray. For those who find it repetitious, it is well to consider that the Word Himself during His agony prayed the same words over. (cf. Matthew 26:44) For those who find it difficult to pray I think that the solution is to practice what Saint Ignatius of Loyola referred to as an awareness "Examen."[7] Before we begin to pray the Rosary we need to stop whatever we are doing or thinking and just realize that we are in God's presence and that He is holding us in being and loving us. We should ask Him to give us a thankful heart as we realize His presence and His love and the gifts He has given to us this day. He has given us His own Holy Spirit to live in us and pray in us and He has given us Mary to be our Mother and the model of how to receive and allow His Word to be born in us.

To begin the Rosary we need to enter the presence of God and of Our Lady in a conscious way; otherwise to whom are we speaking? The Rosary is not a multiplication of words; it is the same words repeated over and over so that instead of focusing on the words we are praying, we may enter into the mystery which we are contemplating. But like every other type of growth, learning to pray the Rosary from the heart is a gradual process; it is not something that we can gain by our own efforts, but rather through learning to receive this prayer as a gift from the Holy Spirit and Our Lady who is His spouse. On May 13, 1917 when Our Lady first appeared at Fatima, Lucia and Jacinta could see her, but Francisco could not. Our Lady said, "Tell him to pray the Rosary and he will see me."[8] As soon as he began to pray the Rosary, Francisco could see Our Lady. Although I have never seen Our Lady with my eyes, ever since I began to pray the Rosary more than 35 years ago, I have seen her with my heart. I know that she is waiting also for your heart.

Chapter Three: Partakers of a Heavenly Calling--Praying the Rosary

"Now we know that for those who love God all things work together unto good, for those who, according to his purpose, are saints through his call" (Romans 8:28).

Two nights after Christmas in 2009, I received a call from my brother telling me that my mother had just died. Although not surprised, I was saddened by this news. At the time of receiving this news I was at St. Charles Children's Home with several of our children. Perceiving my sadness, one of our seven year old girls said to me, "Don't be sad, Sister. Now you can just look into your heart and see your mother there." Thinking about this comment, I realized one day that there is no better way to explain how to pray the Rosary than to say that it is an invitation from Heaven to look into our hearts and see the ones we love there.

Entering this prayer we are called to a deeper vision of the mysteries revealed to us in the Word of God. To make this possible we need to first invoke the Holy Spirit, the author of Scripture, through whose power "the Word was made flesh" (John 1:14) in Mary's womb. As Saint Paul says, "we do not know what we should pray for as we ought but the Spirit Himself pleads for us…" (Romans 8:26)

To understand how to pray the Rosary we have to first know its purpose. Saint John Paul II once said that "the key for interpreting reality is that original sin attempts to abolish Fatherhood."[9] The purpose, then, of every devotion is to remove the obstacles which sin, pain, and death (the fruits of original sin) have placed between us and our Heavenly Father. Because Mary is the Immaculate Conception, she has none of these obstacles. Because she is our Mother, she uses the Rosary as a way to step into our lives and teach us in ever deepening ways how to magnify the Lord and rejoice in God our Savior. (cf. Luke 1:46-47) Our Lady's Immaculate Heart is completely open and vulnerable to the Word of God and so in her heart we hear the Father more clearly and we begin to understand what it means to be "saints through his call." (Romans 8:28)

To begin the Rosary, we make the **Sign of the Cross** and then pray the **Apostles' Creed** on the crucifix. The Creed is like the overture of the Rosary because it contains in concise form the mysteries which will be contemplated. On the first bead we pray the **Our Father**; because it is the Lord's Prayer it allows us to enter into the thoughts of His Heart. While praying the next three **Hail Marys** it is customary to ask for an increase of faith, hope, and love. The **Glory Be** prayer then provides the focus of the Rosary which, like every other devotion, is intended to glorify the Blessed Trinity.

We then choose which of the four sets of Rosary mysteries will be the focus of our meditation. Typically, the Joyful mysteries are prayed on Mondays and Saturdays; the Luminous mysteries are prayed on Thursdays, the Sorrowful mysteries are prayed on Tuesdays and Fridays; and the Glorious mysteries are prayed on Sundays and Wednesdays.

(For those who are just learning the Rosary or who find it beneficial to have pictures relating to the mysteries, I recommend using Sister Mary Agnes' interactive online Rosary. It includes all the words of the Rosary prayers, a different Scriptural verse for each Hail Mary, and a different picture for each mystery. This Rosary can be found at: **www.motherofhealinglove.org**

Each set of Rosary mysteries contains five decades. Each decade begins with the name of the mystery being contemplated, ideally followed by a related passage of Scripture. The **Our Father** is then prayed, followed by 10 **Hail Marys**, and the **Glory Be**. Between each decade the **Fatima Prayer** (taught by Our Lady) is usually prayed. Saint John Paul II recommends that, "the contemplation of the mysteries could better express their full spiritual fruitfulness if an effort were made to conclude each mystery with *a prayer for the fruits specific to that particular mystery*. In this way the Rosary would better express its connection with the Christian life."[10]

At the end of the Rosary, the **Hail Holy Queen** is prayed. The Church also offers special indulgences to those who pray for the intentions of the Pope after they have prayed the Rosary.

But this outside structure of the Rosary is only meant to form the room where we can enter and shut the door and pray to our Father in secret. (cf. Matthew 6:6) As Saint John Paul II explained this, the Rosary "has all the *depth of the Gospel message in its entirety*, of which it can be said to be a compendium…With the Rosary, the Christian people *sits at the school of Mary* and is led to contemplate the beauty on the face of Christ and to experience the depths of his love."[11]

The Rosary prayed from the heart draws us more deeply into the source and summit of the Christian life which is the Holy Mass. According to Saint John Paul II, "Not only does this prayer not conflict with the Liturgy, *it sustains it*, since it serves as an excellent introduction and a faithful echo of the Liturgy, enabling people to participate fully and interiorly in it and to reap its fruits in their daily lives."[12]

Greeting Our Lady with the words "Hail Mary," we need to listen with our hearts for her reply since her greeting has the power to fill us with the Holy Spirit. (cf. Luke 1:41) We can bring all of our concerns to God through the soul of Mary which was pierced with the sword of sorrow that the thoughts of many hearts might be revealed. (cf. Luke 2:35) As Saint John Paul II explained this, the Rosary puts "us in living communion with Jesus through — we might say — the heart of his Mother…"[13]

In this living communion of the Rosary, we become "partakers of a heavenly calling" (Hebrews 3:1) because it is God who is calling us into a deeper communion with Himself and with all the members of the mystical Body of Christ. Through the links of the Rosary I truly am able to look into my heart and see and love my mother, father, and relatives-- both living and dead there.

Words of the Rosary prayers:

Sign of the Cross: In the name of the Father, and of the Son, and of the Holy Spirit. Amen.

Apostles Creed: I believe in God, the Father almighty, Creator of heaven and earth, and in Jesus Christ, his only Son, our Lord, who was conceived by the Holy Spirit, born of the Virgin Mary, suffered under Pontius Pilate, was crucified, died and was buried; he descended into hell; on the third day he rose again from the dead; he ascended into heaven, and is seated at the right hand of God the Father almighty; from there he will come to judge the living and the dead. I believe in the Holy Spirit, the holy catholic Church, the communion of saints, the forgiveness of sins, the resurrection of the body, and life everlasting. Amen.

Our Father: Our Father, who art in Heaven; hallowed by Thy name; Thy kingdom come; Thy will be done on earth as it is in Heaven. Give us this day our daily bread; and forgive us our trespasses as we forgive those who trespass against us, and lead us not into temptation; but deliver us from evil. Amen

Hail Mary: Hail Mary, full of grace, the Lord is with thee. Blessed art thou among women and blessed is the fruit of thy womb, Jesus. Holy Mary, Mother of God, pray for us sinners now and at the hour of our death. Amen

Glory Be: Glory be to the Father, to the Son and to the Holy Spirit. As it was in the beginning, is now and ever shall be, world without end, Amen.

Fatima Prayer: O My Jesus, forgive us our sins, save us from the fires of hell. Lead all souls to Heaven, especially those most in need of Thy mercy.

Hail Holy Queen: Hail, Holy Queen, Mother of Mercy, our life, our sweetness and our hope. To thee do we cry, poor banished children of Eve. To thee do we send up our sighs, mourning and weeping in this valley of tears. Turn then, most gracious advocate, thine eyes of mercy towards us, and after this our exile, show unto us the blessed Fruit of thy womb, Jesus. O clement. O loving, O sweet Virgin Mary.
V. Pray for us, O holy Mother of God
R. That we may be made worthy of the promises of Christ.

Quick View of How to Pray the Rosary

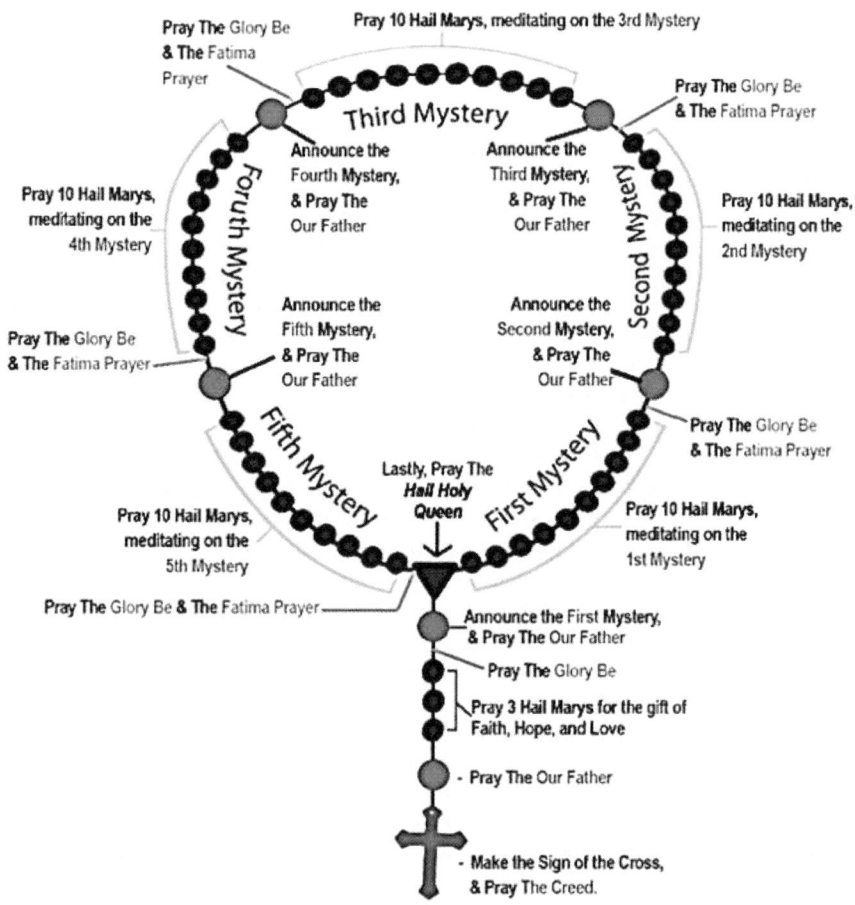

1. While holding the crucifix, make the **Sign of the Cross** and then recite the **Apostles Creed**.

2. Recite the **Our Father** on the first large bead.

3. Recite a **Hail Mary** for an increase of faith, hope, and charity on each of the three small beads.

4. Recite the **Glory Be.**

5. Recite the **Fatima Prayer** (Optional): "O My Jesus, forgive us our sins, save us from the fires of hell. Lead all souls to Heaven, especially those most in need of Thy mercy."

5. Recall the first mystery and recite the **Our Father** on the large bead.

6. On each of the adjacent 10 small beads (also referred to as a decade) recite a **Hail Mary** while reflecting on the mystery.

7. On the next large bead, recite the **Glory Be** and if desired, the **Fatima Prayer**.

8. Each succeeding decade is prayed in a similar manner by recalling the appropriate mystery, reciting the **Our Father** and 10 **Hail Marys**.

9. When the fifth mystery is completed, the Rosary is customarily concluded with the **Hail Holy Queen** and the **Sign of the Cross.**

How to Pray the Rosary
Using This Book

    The essence of the Rosary is meditation on the Word of God which draws us more deeply into the Heart of God and the communion of saints. As an aid to this, I have provided a meditation for each Rosary mystery and I have related one statement that Jesus made about Himself to each mystery. The traditional fruits of each mystery are also listed along with additional Scriptural references. This is by no means an exhaustive list, however; since the whole New Testament relates in some way to the mysteries which are contemplated in the Rosary.

    This book is written as an invitation for you to discover the treasures that are hidden in the Rosary, but don't feel bound to using these particular meditations or to using a particular method. Let the Holy Spirit lead you to what is best for you. God would like to use the Rosary as a means to open His Heart to you and to help you open your heart to Him. In order for this to occur, it is good to set time aside for praying the Rosary, to find a prayer place that is relatively free of distractions, and not to give up, if at first, praying the Rosary seems very difficult. It is wise for those who are just beginning to start by praying just one decade each day and then to gradually build up to a daily five decade Rosary.

Chapter Four: Cause of Our Joy
--The Joyful Mysteries

> "This my joy, therefore, is made full; he must increase, but I must decrease"
> (John 3:29, 30).

Some people appreciate the invention of the GPS more than others do. Although I can attest that it is still possible to get lost even while using a GPS, I know that, despite numerous recalculations, if I follow the directions given, I will eventually reach my destination.

Praying the Joyful Mysteries of the Rosary is like using a spiritual GPS. We are all on a journey together; we have to set eternal joy as our destination in order to reach it successfully. Meditating on the Mysteries, we learn to imitate Our Lady and to listen to her directions in our hearts.

Jesus, for the joy set before Him, endured the cross. (cf. Hebrews 12:2) The Joyful mysteries of the Rosary will help us to stay focused on eternal joy as we endure the crosses of our earthly lives. In the words of Saint John Paul II they will become, "a spiritual itinerary in which Mary acts as Mother, Teacher and Guide, sustaining the faithful by her powerful intercession."[14] Then finally we will rejoice to hear Our Lady say, "Arriving at destination!"

Table 5

Joyful Mysteries	Fruit of the Mystery	"I AM" Statements of Jesus	Other related verses
Annunciation	Humility	"Before Abraham came to be, I am." (John 8:58)	Luke 1:26-38
Visitation	Love of Neighbor	"I am the root and the offspring of David, the bright morning star." (Revelation 22:16)	Luke 1:39-56
Birth of Jesus	Poverty of spirit	"I am the Son of God." (John 10:36)	Luke 2:1-20
Presentation of Jesus in the Temple	Obedience	"I am the door of the sheep." (John 10:7)	Luke 2:22-39
The Finding in the Temple	Joy in finding Jesus	"I am the way, and the truth, and the life." (John 14:6)	Luke 2:41-52

First Joyful Mystery: The Annunciation

"Before Abraham came to be,
I am." (John 8:58)

One time Jesus infuriated his enemies by saying, "Before Abraham came to be I am." (John 8:58) For the Jews, this was the same as saying, "I am God," because "I AM" had been the Jewish Name for God ever since he revealed Himself to Moses in the burning bush. (cf. Ex 3:14) Since Abraham had lived about 1,900 years before Jesus, and since the Jews did not know that God is a Trinity of Persons, they could not understand how this man could say that he was God. Even for us it is shocking to realize that the Second Person of the Trinity united a perfect human nature with his Divinity and became a tiny embryo in Our Lady's womb at the moment she said yes to God's plan.

The first direction Our Lady gives us is to say yes to God. Imagine how joyful Our Lady is because God gave her the grace to say yes. Excuse this mundane example by the daughter of a sportswriter; but just imagine how happy Doug Mientkiewicz is that he didn't drop the ball when he caught it to win the 2004 World Series for the Boston Red Sox! He could've dropped it. Similarly at the Annunciation, Our Lady could have said no. But she said yes. And far more important than winning the World Series, she won the whole world back to God, and earned the title, "Cause of our Joy."

Second Joyful Mystery: The Visitation

"I am the root and offspring of David, the bright morning star." (Rev 22:16)

In the Mystery of the Visitation, we learn to move in the direction of self-giving love, because we see Our Lady taking the initiative to bring God's Healing Love to Elizabeth and her unborn child, Saint John the Baptist. We also learn the power of the Hail Mary, because we know that "Hail" means "Hello." Greeting Our Lady from our hearts will certainly cause her to respond. Meditating on her Visitation, we realize that those who receive her greeting are filled with joy and the Holy Spirit.

What are you worried about today? Why don't you bring it to Jesus and Mary through the Rosary? Our Lady will bring her Son Jesus into the situation that is causing you so much anxiety and when she returns the greeting that you give to her in the Hail Mary, you will be filled with the Holy Spirit. He will help you to see with clarity how to bring His healing love into the situation.

Third Joyful Mystery: The Birth of Jesus

"I am the Son of God." (John 10:36)

When God was born as an infant in Bethlehem, His angels were so filled with exultation that they couldn't refrain from coming down from Heaven to announce to the shepherds this "good news of great joy" and to sing "Glory to God in the highest, and on earth, peace among men of good will." (Luke 2: 10, 14) When you receive a gift that you like very much, you probably keep looking at it and thinking about it. This rejoicing of the angels should teach us to think often about the unimaginably great eternal gift of Christmas.

Jesus is born for us so that we can be born of God. On the first Christmas night, there was no room in the inn for Jesus. "He came unto His own, and His own received Him not. But to as many as received Him, He gave the power of becoming sons of God." (John 1:11) This mystery of becoming incorporated into the Body of Christ as sons in the Son took place when we were baptized. This reality of the Church becoming one Body with Jesus Christ through Baptism is the gift of Christmas.

In the Mystery of the Birth of Jesus, Our Lady directs us to open our hearts to receive her Son and the gift of spiritual childhood. Then the Holy Spirit will be free to cry out "Abba, Father!" (Galatians 4:6) within us. We will find our first love again and we will carry the joy of Christmas into every sad circumstance of life.

Fourth Joyful Mystery:
The Presentation of Jesus in the Temple

"I am the door of the sheep."
(John 10:7)

On the night before He died for us, Jesus prayed that we would know that the Father loves us as He loves Jesus. (cf. John 17: 23) Think about it. How could the Infinite Father, Who has no beginning and has always loved His Son with the perfect Love of the Holy Spirit, love us small sinful creatures, made out of nothing, with the same love as He loves His perfect Son? It can only be because the Son through Baptism has made us one with Himself and has filled us with His Holy Spirit, so that the Father in loving us is loving His Son.

In the Mystery of the Presentation, Joseph and Mary offer the Baby Jesus to the Father in the Temple. Similarly, at every Mass we offer the Son to the Father through the Holy Spirit. When you were little, maybe your mother used to buy gifts for you to give to your other relatives. This is similar to what the Holy Spirit and Our Lady have done for us in giving us Jesus so that we may have a worthy Gift to offer to the Father.

Fifth Joyful Mystery:
The Finding of the Child Jesus in the Temple

"I am the way, and the truth, and the life."
(John 14:6)

After three very anxious days of searching for Him, when Mary and Joseph found the twelve year old Jesus in the temple sitting in the midst of the teachers listening to them and asking them questions, Our Lady asked Him, "'Son, why have you done so to us? Behold, in sorrow thy father and I have been seeking thee.' And he said to them, 'How is it that you sought me? Did you not know that I must be about my Father's business?' And they did not understand the word that he spoke to them." (Luke 2:48-50) Mary and Joseph were the two greatest saints who ever lived and God chose them to be the mother and foster father of the Incarnate Word of God, but even they sometimes did not understand the words of God.

Standing at the top of a very high cliff and looking down makes us feel dizzy; similarly, when we begin to realize the unfathomable depths of the words of God we can feel overwhelmed. But Jesus tells us, "Seek and you shall find," (Matthew 7:7) because, just like the manna for the Israelites adapted itself to everyone's taste, the words of God adapt to our limited capacity. The more we enter into the heart of our Mother Mary, who "kept in mind all these things pondering them in her heart," (Luke 2:19) the more our capacity for the words of God will expand.

Chapter Five: Doorway to the Depths of the Heart of Christ
The Luminous Mysteries

"You have kept the good wine until now." (John 2:10)

On October 13, 2010, when the 33 Chilean miners were rescued after having been trapped underground for more than two months, they were each given a specially designed pair of sunglasses to prevent their eyes from being damaged by being too suddenly exposed to the brightness of the sun. Although "God is Light," (1 John 1:5) we tend to be more accustomed to our own darkened perceptions of Him. This is due to the effects of original and actual sin.

Meditating with Our Lady on the Luminous mysteries of the Rosary provides a way for the eyes of our hearts to become gradually more and more accustomed to absorbing "the Light of the World" (John 8:12) into our everyday interior lives. Being without original or actual sin, Our Lady became the capacity, through the overshadowing of the Holy Spirit, for "the Light of the World." (John 8:12) Our Lady mothers us by reflecting God's brilliance in a way that makes it more accessible to our limited capacities and that is why Scripture describes her as "fair as the moon." (Song of Songs 6:10)

Table 6a

Luminous Mysteries	Fruit of the Mystery	"I AM" Statements of Jesus	Other related verses
Baptism of Jesus	Openness to the Holy Spirit	"The woman said to him, I know that Messiah is coming…Jesus said to her, 'I who speak with thee am he.'" (Jn 4:25)	Mt 3:13-17 Mk 1:9-11 Lk 3:21-22 Jn 1:29-34
Wedding Feast at Cana	To Jesus through Mary	"I am the vine, you are the branches." (Jn 15:5)	Jn 2:1-12
Proclamation of the Kingdom of God	Repentance and Trust in God	"I am a king. This is why I was born, and why I have come into the world, to bear witness to the truth." (Jn 18:37)	Mt 10:1-42 Mk 1:15; 2:3-13 Lk 7:47-48, 9:1-6 Jn 18:33-37, 20:22-23

Table 6b

Luminous Mysteries	Fruit of the Mystery	"I AM" Statements of Jesus	Other Related Verses
The Transfiguration	Desire for holiness	"Father, I will that where I am, they also whom thou hast given me may be with me; in order that they may behold my glory." (John 17:24)	Mt 17:1-13 Mk 9:1-12 Lk 9:28-36 Jn 1:14 2 Peter 1:16-21
The Institution of the Eucharist	Adoration	"I am the living bread that has come down from heaven. If anyone eat of this bread he shall live forever; and the bread that I will give is my flesh for the life of the world." (John 6:51, 52)	Mt 26:26-29 Mark 14:22-25 Luke 22:14-20 John 6:22-70, 13:1 1 Cor 11:23-26

Saint John Paul II added these Mysteries of Light (Luminous Mysteries) into the Rosary in October 2002. He cited several reasons for adding these Mysteries:

1. to remedy the fact that "of the many mysteries of Christ's life, only a few are indicated by the Rosary in the traditional 15 decade form";

2. "to bring out fully the Christological depth of the Rosary";

3. "to broaden it to include the mysteries of Christ's public ministry between his Baptism and his Passion";

4. to aid in contemplating "important aspects of the person of Christ as the definitive revelation of God";

5. to highlight that it is in "the years of his public ministry that the mystery of Christ is most evidently a mystery of light";

6. to enable the Rosary to become more fully a "compendium of the Gospel";

7. to provide "a meditation on certain particularly significant moments in his public ministry";

8. "to give it fresh life and to enkindle renewed interest in the Rosary's place within Christian spirituality as a true doorway to the depths of the Heart of Christ, ocean of joy and of light, of suffering and of glory";

9. to illustrate that "each of these mysteries is a revelation of the Kingdom now present in the very person of Jesus" [15]

As we enter the "doorway to the depths of the Heart of Christ" through the Luminous Mysteries, we are entering the wine cellar where someday all the desires of our hearts for intimacy and understanding will be fully satisfied.

First Luminous Mystery:
The Baptism of Jesus

"The woman said to him, 'I know that Messiah is coming…Jesus said to her, 'I who speak with thee am he.'" (John 4:25)

In this mystery the Holy Spirit descended upon Jesus in the form of a dove and the Father spoke saying, "This is my beloved Son, with whom I am well pleased." (Matthew 3:17) God the Son received the Father's anointing with the Holy Spirit at His Baptism in the Jordan so that all the members of His Body (who would later be incorporated into Him through the Sacrament of Baptism) could share in His role as prophet, priest, and king.

Through His Baptism in the Jordan and His passion, death, and resurrection, Jesus gave us the gift of sacramental Baptism. (cf. Luke 12:50) The Church calls Baptism "the gateway to the life in the Spirit."[16] The baptismal candle which we received at our baptism was lighted from the Easter Vigil candle. This symbolizes that through our rebirth by water and the Holy Spirit (cf. John 3:5) we became the beloved sons and daughters of God, sent as members of the Body of Christ to be the "the light of the world." (Matthew 5:14) When we pray this mystery, we should ask Our Lady to help us regain the light of a true understanding of our identity and mission as the beloved sons and daughters of God.

Second Luminous Mystery:
The Wedding Feast at Cana

"I am the vine, you are the branches."
(John 15:5)

At the wedding feast of Cana, when the wine ran out, Our Lady interceded to her Son, Jesus, and He told the waiters to fill six (approximately 15-20 gallon) stone water jars with water. He then changed the substance of the water into such good wine that when the chief steward tasted it he said, "Every man at first sets forth the good wine, and when they have drunk freely, then that which is poorer. But thou hast kept the good wine until now." (John 2:10) Through this miracle Jesus "manifested His glory; and His disciples believed in Him." (John 2:11)

This miracle of changing water into wine foreshadowed the hour of His Eucharistic miracle when He would change wine into His Precious Blood. As Pope Benedict XVI explains this, "Just as at His mother's request Jesus gives a sign that anticipates His hour, and at the same time directs our gaze toward it, so too He does the same thing ever anew in the Eucharist. Here, in response to the Church's prayer, the Lord anticipates His return; He comes already now; He celebrates the marriage feast with us here and now. In so doing, He lifts us out of our own time toward the coming 'hour.'"[17]

Praying this mystery, we should ask Our Lady to obtain the new wine of the Holy Spirit from her Son for us. Then we will be able to "taste and see that the Lord is good!" (Psalm 34:8) Instead of ignoring our invitation to the wedding, we will realize that at every moment God has always "kept the good wine until now." (John 2:10) Because He is an Infinite Subject, there is no limit, and there never will be, to how deeply we can drink of His beauty, love, and sweetness.

Third Luminous Mystery:
The Proclamation of the Kingdom of God

"I am a king. This is why I was born,
and why I have come into the world,
to bear witness to the truth." (John 18:37)

Jesus began his public preaching by saying, "The time is fulfilled, and the kingdom of God is at hand; repent, and believe in the gospel." (Mark 1:15) With these words He shows us that the key to receiving the Good News of the Kingdom of God is repentance. Just as a beam of sunlight illuminates the dust particles that are in the air, the Light of God's Holy Spirit illuminates the aspects of our interior lives that are most in need of His merciful healing love. The deeper the level of our repentance, the more we will be able to receive and proclaim the Kingdom of God.

On Easter Sunday night, Jesus gave the Apostles and their successors the power to forgive sins (cf. John 20:22-23) so that no matter what sins we have committed, the power of Resurrection is always available to us through the Sacrament of Reconciliation. When we have been forgiven, and when we have forgiven others, then God can use us to proclaim the Kingdom of His merciful love. Seeing people change from being selfish to being selfless attracts others to the Kingdom of God; it is like seeing water change into wine.

Fourth Luminous Mystery: The Transfiguration

"Father, I will that where I am, they also whom thou has given me may be with me; in order that they may behold my glory." (John 17:24)

Saint John Paul II called the Transfiguration "the mystery of light par excellence" because, "In contemplating Christ's face we become open to receiving the mystery of Trinitarian life, experiencing ever anew the love of the Father and delighting in the joy of the Holy Spirit."[18] Jesus is one Divine Person with two natures. During His earthly life Jesus kept the glory of His Divine Nature hidden beneath the appearance of His human nature. At the Transfiguration, He allowed his apostles Peter, James, and John to see His face shining like the sun (cf. Matthew 17:2) so that they would become certain of His Divinity.

Later, in writing about this event, Saint Peter compared the revelation of the glory of Jesus Christ that he had seen at the Transfiguration with the revelation of the glory of Jesus Christ that is revealed in Sacred Scripture. Speaking of meditating on the mysteries revealed to us through Scripture, Saint Peter says, "You will do well to pay attention to this as to a lamp shining in a dark place, until the day dawns and the morning star rises in your hearts." (cf. 2 Peter 1:16-21) The primary purpose of meditating on every Rosary mystery is to illuminate for us at ever deeper levels what Saint Peter refers to as "the words of everlasting life." (John 6:69)

Fifth Luminous Mystery:
The Institution of the Eucharist

"I am the living bread that has come
down from heaven. If anyone eat of
this bread he shall live forever,
and the bread that I will give is my flesh
for the life of the world." (John 6:51, 52)

On the night before He died, Jesus instituted the Sacrament of the Eucharist so that the whole communion of saints could live united with Him through this astonishing gift. He continues at every Mass, through the power of the Holy Spirit given to His priests, to change bread and wine into His Sacred Body and Blood. In meditating on this mystery, we should be particularly grateful to Our Lady, who through her yes to the Holy Spirit, conceived the Body of Christ and gave Him to us so that we could receive His promise: "He who eats my flesh and drinks my blood has eternal life, and I will raise him up at the last day. For my flesh is food indeed, and my blood is drink indeed. He who eats my flesh and drinks my blood abides in me, and I in him." (John 6:54-56)

In his *Theology of the Body*, Saint John Paul II explained the connection between the love of husband and wife and the love of Christ for His Bride — the Church — by citing this verse from Ephesians: "For this cause a man shall leave his father and mother, and cleave to his wife; and the two shall become one flesh. This is a great mystery — I mean in reference to Christ and to the Church." (Ephesians 5:31, 32) As a husband gives the gift of his body to his wife and she receives him and returns the gift of her body, so Jesus at Mass gives his Bride the gift of His own Eucharistic Body; He expects those He has incorporated into Himself to return the gift through self-giving love.[19] In the Eucharist, God has given us a foreshadowing of His desire to unite us as one people with Himself and to fill us with joy for all eternity.

Chapter Six: The Immeasurable Riches of His Grace
The Sorrowful Mysteries

"If you knew the gift of God, and who it is who says to you, 'Give me to drink,' you, perhaps, would have asked of Him, and He would have given you living water" (John 4:10).

On October 8, 2010, *The Buffalo News* reported that an Italian art historian thinks that a painting discovered recently in Niagara Falls, New York may actually be an original unfinished work by Michelangelo. The painting belongs to a retired airline pilot who, not knowing its origin, had left it behind a couch for several years. If proven authentic, this painting could be worth up to 300 million dollars.[20]

Yet we have a treasure that is worth far more! It is "the immeasurable riches of His grace in kindness toward us in Christ Jesus. For by grace you have been saved through faith; and this is not your own doing, it is the gift of God." (Ephesians 2:7, 8) Saint Peter tells us that the Blood of Christ, by which we were ransomed from eternal death, is worth more than any amount of silver or gold (cf. 1 Peter 1:18, 19).

There is nothing of more value than the Cross of Jesus Christ for through it death, suffering, and sin have been destroyed. This infinite treasure won for us by Jesus in His Passion is our inheritance either to relish at ever deeper levels, or to neglect like an unremembered masterpiece behind a couch (cf. Mark 4:21).

Meditating with Our Lady on the Sorrowful mysteries of the Rosary allows us to draw from these unfathomable riches of Christ the strength to view every event of our lives from within the context of the Infinite value that Jesus assigned to each of us by laying down His life for us. The Sorrowful mysteries occurred in less than 24 hours of time, yet they continue by their mysterious efficacy to profoundly influence every moment of history.

Table 7a

Sorrowful Mysteries	Fruit of the Mystery	"I AM" Statements of Jesus	Other Related Verses
Agony in the Garden	Sorrow for sin	"Jesus answered, 'I have told you that I am he. If, therefore, you seek me, let these go their way.'" (John 18:8)	Mt 26:36-55 Mk 14:32-52 Lk 22:39-53 Jn 18:1-11
Scourging at the Pillar	Purity	"I am the good shepherd." (John 10:11)	Mt 27:26 Mk 15:15 Jn 19:1
Crowning with Thorns	Moral Courage	"And Jesus said to him, 'I am. And you shall see the Son of Man sitting at the right hand of the Power and coming with the clouds of heaven.'" (Mark 14:62)	Mt 27:29 Mk 15:17 Jn 19:2

Table 7b

Sorrowful Mysteries	Fruit of the Mystery	"I AM" Statements of Jesus	Other Related Verses
Carrying of the Cross	Patience	"…I am meek and humble of heart; and you will find rest for our souls. For my yoke is easy, and my burden light." (Mt 11:29-30)	Mt 27:31-32 Mk 15:20-22 Lk 23:26-32 Jn 19:17
Crucifixion	Perseverance	"I am the First and the Last, and he who lives; I was dead, and behold, I am living forevermore; and I have the keys of death and of hell." (Rev 1:17,18)	Mt 27:35-50 Mk 15:24-37 Lk 23:33-46 Jn 19:18-30

First Sorrowful Mystery:
The Agony in the Garden

"Jesus answered, 'I have told you that I am He. If, therefore, you seek me, let these go their way.'" (John 18:8)

Suffering, sin, death, and the destruction of our relationship with the Father entered the world when Adam and Eve disobeyed in the Garden of Eden. It was to reverse all this that Jesus, the Second Person of the Trinity, entered the Garden of Olives, took upon Himself the guilt of all of our sins, and offered His life to the Father to ransom us from death. Seeing in advance the lack of response that this unsurpassable act of love would receive from so many people made this offering excruciatingly difficult for Jesus. He begged the Father to take it away from Him, and He sweat blood in the effort that it cost Him to pray, "Nevertheless not my will, but Thine, be done." (Luke 22:42-44)

In the struggle of Jesus, He reveals the certainty that "God is Love" (1 John 4:8) and that He wills our salvation. Uniting our hearts to Jesus in His Agony allows us to see all of our own sufferings in the context of God healing the world.

Second Sorrowful Mystery: The Scourging at the Pillar

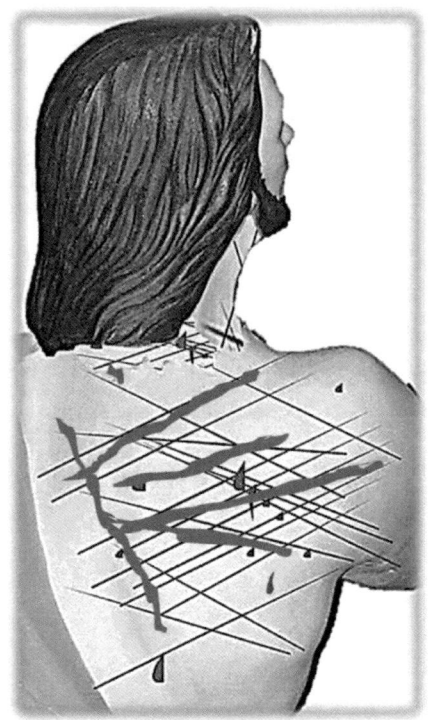

"I am the good shepherd" (John 10:11).

Saint Peter tells us, "By His wounds you have been healed." (1 Peter 2:24) In this mystery, we meditate on the terrible bloody scourging which Jesus underwent in His innocent Body so that the damage sin had done to all humanity could be repaired. Because Jesus is the Second Person of the Trinity, the sufferings He endured in His perfect human nature have an infinite value.

Of all people who ever lived on the earth, only Jesus could make a worthy offering to the Father, because only He is God the Son. When we meditate on this mystery, we should unite our small sufferings to His; then, just like a drop of water falling into the ocean, our sufferings will take on an immortal value.

Third Sorrowful Mystery:
The Crowning with Thorns

"And Jesus said to him, 'I am.
And you shall see the Son of Man sitting
at the right hand of the Power and coming
with the clouds of heaven.'" (Mark 14:62)

In this mystery, Jesus, who is the King of Kings, allowed Himself to be crowned with thorns, spat upon, and mocked as if He were only pretending to be a king. Although Jesus allowed His outward appearance to become totally disfigured, (cf. Isaiah 53:2-7) His identity as the Second Person of the Trinity, True God from True God, remained the same.

Meditating on this illustrates why Jesus told us not to judge by appearances. (cf. John 7:24) Each of us is a unique and irreplaceable image of God. Sin disfigures us and makes it difficult to perceive this image; but Jesus by allowing himself to be mocked and scorned urges us to see beyond outward appearances and to perceive in each person the dignity of a child of God.

Fourth Sorrowful Mystery:
The Carrying of the Cross

"I am meek and humble of heart;
and you will find rest for your souls.
For my yoke is easy, and
my burden light." (Matthew 11:29-30)

Saint Bernard taught people to venerate the wound in the shoulder of Jesus because Jesus had revealed that this wound inflicted by the heavy weight of the Cross was His greatest unrecorded suffering. Jesus promised to greatly bless those who venerate this wound. Meditating on how painful was the Cross Jesus carried on His shoulder helps us to receive the grace to be more patient with the difficulties and crosses of our own daily lives. When we enter through the Rosary into Mary's contemplation of Jesus, God is able to superimpose the eternal significance of these mysteries onto the seemingly insignificant events of our daily lives.

The way Saint John Paul II explains this is that, "Mary's contemplation is above all *a remembering*. We need to understand this word in the biblical sense of remembrance (*zakar*) as a making present of the works brought about by God in the history of salvation...This making present comes about above all in the Liturgy: what God accomplished centuries ago did not only affect the direct witnesses of those events; it continues to affect people in every age with its gift of grace. To some extent this is also true of every other devout approach to those events: to "remember" them in a spirit of faith and love is to be open to the grace which Christ won for us by the mysteries of his life, death and resurrection."[21]

Fifth Sorrowful Mystery: The Crucifixion

"I am the First and the Last, and He who lives; I was dead, and behold, I am living forevermore; and I have the keys of death and of hell." (Revelation 1:17, 18)

Dying on the Cross, Jesus left us the gift of His Mother Mary to be our Mother and the gift of His Holy Spirit to live in us and guide us into all Truth. He offered His Mercy to every person who would choose to receive it, (cf. Luke 23:34) and by allowing Himself to feel totally abandoned by the Father (cf. Matthew 27:46) He reached the ultimate depths of human pain and provided hope for the despairing.

After Jesus died, Saint John, who was an eyewitness told us that "one of the soldiers opened his side with a lance, and immediately there came out blood and water….these things came to pass that the Scripture might be fulfilled, 'Not a bone of him shall you break.' And again another Scripture says, 'they shall look upon him whom they have pierced.'" (John 19:34, 36, 37) The first Scripture Saint John cites (Exodus 12:46) identifies Jesus as the Paschal Lamb Who became the perfect Sacrifice for sin. The second Scripture he cites (Zechariah 12:10) refers to the opening of the Sacred Heart of Jesus which coincided with the revealing of the Holy of Holies in the Temple at Jerusalem when "the curtain of the temple was torn in two from top to bottom." (Matthew 27:51). Just 3 verses later Zechariah prophesied that "On that day, there shall be open….a fountain to purify from sin and uncleanness." (Zechariah 13:1) This fountain from the Heart of Jesus is considered by the Fathers of the Church to be the origin of the sacramental life of the Church. As Eve came forth from the side of Adam as he slept, (cf. Genesis 2: 21-23) so the Church came forth from the side of Jesus as He slept in death.

Meditating on this mystery allows us to see that, through the gifts of Baptism and the Holy Eucharist (which came forth as blood and water from the Sacred Heart of Jesus), the Church truly is the Bride of Christ, "members of his body, made from his flesh and from his bones." (Ephesians 5:29-32) This is not merely a symbolic reality. Jesus died on the Cross to make us one Body with Himself.

Chapter Seven: Clothed with Power from on High
The Glorious Mysteries

"And behold, I send the promise of my Father upon you; but wait here in the city, until you are clothed with power from on high." (Luke 24:49)

Moviemakers use trailers to captivate their prospective audiences and draw them irresistibly into the story. The Glorious mysteries are like trailers that give us a preview of the amazing future that Jesus has gone ahead to prepare for us. Psalm 68:18 describes well the magnetism of these mysteries: "You have ascended on high, taken captives, received men as gifts — even rebels; the Lord God enters his dwelling." According to Saint John Paul II, the "glorious mysteries, ought to lead the faithful to an ever greater appreciation of their new life in Christ, lived in the heart of the Church."[22]

The more we appreciate our new life in Christ, the more we will fall in love with Him and the greater will be our capacity to receive Him. This is the key reason why the Rosary is such a powerful prayer. We are uniting our small love and appreciation to the Immaculate Mother's immeasurable love and appreciation, and so we enter under the shadow of the Holy Spirit who espoused her.

Table 8

Glorious Mysteries	Fruit of the Mystery	"I AM" Statements of Jesus	Other Related Verses
Resurrection	Faith	"I am the Resurrection and the life." (Jn 11:25)	Mt 28:1-15 Mk 16:1-18 Lk 24:1-49 Jn 20:1-23
Ascension	Hope	"I am in my Father, and you in me, and I in you." (John 14:20)	Mk 16:19-20 Lk 24:50-52 Acts 1:1-11
Descent of the Holy Spirit	Love	"I am the Light of the world." (John 8:12)	Acts 2:1-41
Assumption of Our Lady into Heaven	Grace of a Happy Death	"I am coming again, and I will take you to myself; that where I am, there you also may be." (John 14:3)	Song of Songs 2:10
Crowning of the Blessed Virgin Mary as Queen of Heaven and Earth	Trust in Mary's intercession	"I am he who searches desires and hearts, and I will give to each of you according to your works." (Rev 2:23)	Rev 12:1

First Glorious Mystery: The Resurrection

"I am the Resurrection and the life."
(John 11:25)

Everyone who attends the funeral of a loved one does so with the hope of seeing that person alive again someday. This hope of Resurrection was planted in our souls at our Baptism. On the night before Jesus died, He promised his apostles, "and you therefore have sorrow now; but I will see you again, and your heart shall rejoice, and your joy no one shall take from you" (John 16:22).

The whole power of the Gospel lies in this hope of Resurrection. When Adolf Reinach was killed in World War I, it was his widow Anna's witness of serene hope that led her friend Edith Stein to take her first steps out of atheism towards Christianity. Eighty-one years later on October 11, 1998, Edith Stein was canonized as Saint Teresa Benedicta of the Cross.

Jesus destroyed the power of death and sin when He rose from the dead on the third day after His Crucifixion. The Liturgy of the Easter season reminds us that "the joy of the resurrection renews the whole world." We experience this joy of Resurrection in the Sacrament of Reconciliation -- an Easter gift which Jesus gave to His Church. It was on Easter Sunday night that He appeared to His Apostles and breathed on them and said, "Receive the Holy Spirit; whose sins you shall forgive, they are forgiven them; and whose sins you shall retain, they are retained." (John 20:22-23)

Meditating on the glorious Resurrection of Jesus from the dead on the third day after His Crucifixion enkindles our own hope of resurrection. We begin to share with Our Lady, the Apostles, and the other holy women this joy of the Resurrection which renews the whole world and which no one can take away.

Second Glorious Mystery: The Ascension of Jesus into Heaven

"I am in my Father, and you in me, and I in you." (John 14:20)

In the garden where He had been buried, the Risen Jesus appeared to Saint Mary Magdalene on Easter morning and told her, "Go to my brethren and say to them, 'I ascend to my Father and your Father, to my God and your God.'" (John 20:17) By these words Jesus declared the restoration of the relationship with the Father. Forty days after His resurrection, Jesus ascended into Heaven and is now seated at the right Hand of the Father interceding for us.

St. Paul tells us, "If you have risen with Christ, seek the things that are above, where Christ is seated at the right hand of God. Mind the things that are above, not the things that are on earth." (Colossians 3;1,2). While we are on earth, we are burdened by continual distractions and we find it difficult to focus on the reality that God has "seated us together in heaven in Christ Jesus." (Ephesians 2:6) The Rosary provides a space in our consciousness where we can become more aware of these stupendous realities and enter through the Hearts of Jesus and Mary into an ever deepening intimacy with our Heavenly Father.

Third Glorious Mystery:
The Descent of the Holy Spirit

"I am the Light of the world." (John 8:12)

Before He ascended into Heaven, Jesus told His apostles, "I send forth upon you the promise of my Father. But wait here in the city, until you are clothed with power from on high." (Luke 24:49) After witnessing His Ascension, the Apostles returned to Jerusalem and spent the next nine days (the original novena) united with Our Lady and the other holy women asking God for the Gift of His Spirit.

When the Holy Spirit came on Pentecost morning, He filled the Apostles with so much joy that some of the people said, "They are full of new wine." (Acts 2:13) New wine is a symbol of the Holy Spirit because it is only through Him that we are able to know God and to taste His sweetness. Without the Holy Spirit, the Rosary is just a collection of words and ideas because "the things of God no one knows but the Spirit of God." (1 Corinthians 2:11). But with the Holy Spirit meditation on these mysteries draws us into the wine cellar of God's amazing Love.

Uniting with Mary in prayer, as we do whenever we pray the Rosary from our hearts, greatly increases our capacity to receive the Holy Spirit. At the Annunciation, Mary was told that, "The Holy Spirit will come upon you, and the power of the Most High will overshadow you," (Luke 1:35) and Jesus Christ was conceived. At Pentecost, the Holy Spirit overshadowed the Church united with Mary, and the Body of Christ was born. Pentecost is considered to be the birthday of the Church. Saint Peter's first sermon on Pentecost brought 3,000 new members into the Body of Christ through the Sacrament of Baptism. (cf. Acts 2:41) It is through the Holy Spirit that we are able to "understand the gifts bestowed on us by God." (1 Corinthians 2:12) These gifts include the Mysteries we contemplate in the Rosary.

Fourth Glorious Mystery: The Assumption of Mary into Heaven

"I am coming again, and I will take you to myself; that where I am, there you also may be." (John 14:3)

At the Last Supper Jesus promised, "And if I go and prepare a place for you, I am coming again, and I will take you to myself; that where I am, there you also may be." (John 14:3) In the mystery of the Assumption, we see Jesus fulfill this promise in His Mother whom He assumed body and soul into Heaven at the end of her earthly life. Mary is in Heaven, but she desires that we live in her heart, like most children live in their mother's hearts. She is not an abstract symbol, but a mother with a beating heart who is waiting for us.

God uses what He has done for Mary individually as a sign to teach us what He desires to do for the whole Church — to draw us joyfully toward our destined reunion with Jesus and with all those loved ones whom He has already taken to Himself.

**Fifth Glorious Mystery:
The Crowning of Mary as
Queen of Heaven and Earth**

"I am he who searches desires and hearts,
and I will give to each of you according
to your works." (Revelation 2:23)

The Church Fathers believed that what could be said of Mary could be said of the Church and vice versa. As Saint John Paul II explained this, "Crowned in glory — as she appears in the last glorious mystery — Mary shines forth as Queen of the Angels and Saints, the anticipation and the supreme realization" of the Church in glory.[23] Meditating on how God blessed Mary's cooperation with his plan and brought her from being a poor unknown teenager in an obscure town (at the time of the Annunciation) to being the Queen of Heaven and Earth whom all generations will call blessed (cf. Luke.1:48), draws us toward a deeper cooperation with God's plans in our individual lives.

Jesus once said, "The kingdom of heaven is like a king who made a marriage feast for his son. And he sent his servants to call in those invited to the marriage feast, but they would not come" (Matthew 22:2-3). This marriage feast of the kingdom of heaven has already begun in our hearts and it will reach its consummation in eternity. God has made Mary Queen of Heaven and Earth and set her as a sign for us (cf. Revelation 12:1-2) to help us hear and respond to His invitation, "Everything is ready. Come to the marriage feast" (Matthew 22:4).

"For I am sure that neither death, nor life, nor angels, nor principalities, nor things present, nor things to come, nor powers, nor height, nor depth, nor any other creature, will be able to separate us from the love of God which is in Christ Jesus our Lord." (Romans 8:38)

Chapter Eight: At the Hour of Our Death
--Intercessory Power of the Rosary

Each time we pray the Rosary, we ask Our Lady 53 times to pray for us at the hour of our death. I was grieved that I hadn't been present at my mother's death, until one day a hospice nurse told me that she had been present at the death of an elderly woman who had loved the Rosary. The nurse said she could feel the power of all the prayers the woman had prayed for the hour of her death. Then I knew that somehow I had been present at my mother's death, because the prayers we pray for one another enter the Presence of God — who is not confined by time.

Praying the Rosary is like taking out an eternal life insurance policy on ourselves and on our loved ones. It is such a powerful policy, that God can use even a Rosary prayed after another person's death to help the person die a happy death. As Saint Padre Pio (one of the Saints that Saint John Paul II pointed out for his great love for the Rosary[24]) explained this, "For the Lord, the past does not exist; the future does not exist. Everything is an eternal present...even now I can pray for the happy death of my great-grandmother!"

The Story of Adam Keenan

The day after Adam Keenan (age 20) died suddenly of cardiac arrest, his mother's first cousin, John, began to pray a Rosary every day for him. It would seem that God took these Rosaries prayed after Adam's death (along with all of Adam's own prayers during his lifetime and those of his family and friends) and applied them in a dramatic way to help Adam and his family at the moment of his death.

Adam was a college student who played baseball for the University of Lowell; in the summer he joined the Seacoast Maverick's team in Rochester, New Hampshire. After their first practice at their home field on June 6, 2011, Adam and his teammates were listening to their coach. Adam was kneeling on one knee, when suddenly he began to have a seizure and fell backwards. Despite receiving immediate medical intervention Adam soon died of cardiac arrest. It was a little bit after 7:30 p.m.

At 7:30 p.m. after attending the city track meet, I was leaving the Spaulding High School track (which is adjacent to the baseball field) with Judith (age 11), Anna (age 7), and Regina (age 6) — three of the children from St. Charles Children's Home. As we were leaving the track to go to our car, I heard the announcer twice ask the nurse from the city track meet to please go down to the baseball field. I looked over to the left; about 60 yards away I saw people kneeling around someone on the ground on the dugout side of the first baseline at the adjacent baseball field. Right away I asked the girls to pray with me for that person and we began to pray. As soon as I began to pray, I felt that the person was dying. I tried to push this thought away; but I asked Jesus that if the person was dying to please have mercy on him. We were walking through the gate of the track then and I had no intention of going over closer to see what was happening. Our car was parked far up to the right and I know that we didn't walk over to the baseball field which was to our left; but it must've been at that point that I remember standing quite close to the people who were working on Adam.

What I remember is standing about 12 yards away from the people who were kneeling around Adam and they were slightly below me. I had such a strong urge to go down and pray right there with them, but I knew that I couldn't do that because of the children who were with me. I even considered bringing the children up closer with me to pray, but then I knew that they were too young for me to do that. I clearly remember this interior argument. What I also remember was that I was completely focused on that scene and everything else around me was silent. I don't remember seeing any grass and I don't remember any cars being around me then and I am certain that there was no fence in front of me. Judith also remembers being close to the people who were working on Adam, and that there was no fence in front of us. Anna and Regina do not have clear memories of this scene.

The next thing I remember was walking by the community center up to the car. This is probably 150 yards away from where Adam was lying, but I don't remember walking the distance in between at all. I know that I was praying in tongues, because Judith asked me what I was doing and I remember explaining to her that tongues is the language of the Holy Spirit. Then we got into the car; as we were saying our traveling prayer to ask the angels for a safe journey, Regina interrupted the prayer to point out a huge cloud that was above where Adam was lying; it looked just like a dog jumping. Sometimes when people ask if a cloud looks like this or that, you have to try to imagine what they are seeing, but this cloud was not like that — it was definitely a dog jumping. (It is interesting that this cloud appeared in the right field sky where Adam, being left handed, would have hit a home run.)

I know that this cloud was a gift from God, because it led to my contacting the Keenan family and becoming friends with them and learning that Adam really loved his dog; but it was only several days later after carefully thinking through the events of that night, that I realized that God had intervened in another amazing way as Adam was dying.

The two times that I had been up at the track since June 6, I had been with the Keenans both times, and neither time could I figure out where we had been standing on the night of Adam's death. This is because I knew we hadn't been on the baseball field and the field is fenced all around and quite a bit above the parking lot, so if we were in the parking lot, how could we have seen the people working on Adam as if they were a little below us and were not behind a fence? Also if Adam was lying beside the first baseline, the exit of the track is at least 60 yards away from there and we would have been turning in the opposite direction as we entered the parking lot to walk toward our car. I know I didn't say to the girls, "Let's go over closer to see what is happening," and it is not my personality to enter into a scene like that, because I would have been thinking that I shouldn't get in the way of the medical personnel and that I could pray just as effectively from a distance.

On July 31, I went back up to the track right before the Mavericks' last home game, because I wanted to confirm that there was no natural explanation of how we could have been so close to Adam that night. I talked with Chris and Craig, two of the coaches, who were there that night, and they showed me where Adam had been lying. It was just where I thought it had been! So I looked over to where I know that I was standing that night in relation to Adam and about 5 yards away there was a low fence and then a set of bleachers, and then another much higher fence behind it. Then I knew for sure that God had intervened in an amazing way to bring us into Adam's presence to pray for him as he was dying. As if to confirm that this gift was associated with the Rosary, David Hoyt, the owner of the Seacoast Mavericks, told me that before the July 31 game, he had been walking across the baseball field, thinking of all the events that had occurred, and he looked down and found a broken rosary lying on the ground between second base and the pitcher's mound. No one knows where it came from or how it got there.

Then just five days before the second anniversary of Adam's death, his mother, Audrey received another confirmation that this was indeed a miracle of the Rosary. Audrey was walking around the field in Lowell, MA where her son had spent so many hours playing baseball. As she tells the story:

"As I approached the batting cages that Adam called his second home, I couldn't help but wish that Adam was there practicing with his dad. I remembered that Michael and Adam had been there the day prior to Adam leaving for Rochester, NH to meet his team and coaches for the Mavericks. As the tears rolled down my face and I passed the batting cages I found a homemade wooden rosary on the dirt track. I couldn't believe my eyes, I picked up the rosary and looked around to see if anyone was here and I was the only one at the track. This rosary was not broken (just dirty). As I continued my walk around the track with the rosary clenched in the hand, I couldn't believe that no one else had picked up this rosary. The prior night was beautiful; there had been a baseball game and I am sure that the park had been full of people! As I continued I knew that the rosary was meant for me!"[25]

Adam Keenan

I thought of a story that the Keenans had told me illustrating Adam's kindness. One day he and his girlfriend had stopped to talk with a man whose nickname is O.G. and then they had taken him out to lunch. This had made O.G. very happy.

Because he suffers from a brain injury, it is not easy for O.G. to put things into words, but he was very grieved by Adam's sudden death. He came to Adam's wake and took one of the holy cards and held it to his heart, then he held it to Adam's sister Christine's heart, and he told her that Adam would be living in their hearts. And this is the truth. Although the Keenans were not physically present with Adam when he died, God put us there as proxies to remind them and all of us that in the communion of His Son's Sacred Heart we really do live within one another's hearts.

This is the love that is stronger than death. It is the Father's answer to the prayer of the Heart of Jesus, "that all may be one, even as thou, Father, in me and I in thee; that they also may be one in us" (John 17:21).The reason that the Rosary has the power to connect hearts and even generations is that it is a meditation that leads us into the Heart of God. To pray it from the heart is to plant seeds in eternity, because the source and substance of the Rosary are the words of God of which Jesus said, "The seed is the word of God," (Luke 8:11) and "Heaven and Earth will pass away, but my words will not pass away." (Matthew 24:35)

Conclusion

As we end this overview of the Rosary, it is important to realize that, with meditating on the Rosary mysteries we will always only be at the beginning since we are dealing with an Infinite Subject. As Saint John Paul II explained: "Every individual event in the life of Christ, as narrated by the Evangelists, is resplendent with the Mystery that surpasses all understanding (cf. Ephesians 3:19): the Mystery of the Word made flesh, in whom 'all the fullness of God dwells bodily.' (Colossians 2:9)"[26] Because there is no limit to the Mystery of God, there is no limit to how deeply one can enter into the Rosary, since ultimately it is a meditation on the Infinite. But our capacities are so limited! This is why consecrating ourselves to Jesus through Mary is so beneficial. In the Heart of our Mother Mary, our small sinful hearts are absorbed into her Immaculate capacity; we become the new wineskins able to receive the new wine of the Holy Spirit, and we become the brothers and sisters and mothers of Christ (cf. Matthew 12:50).

The Rosary is the key to the wine cellar of the Heart of Jesus. It is the desire of His Heart to reveal the Father to us, so that even here on Earth we will begin to enjoy a little of the intimacy that Adam and Eve had with the Heavenly Father in the garden. In the words of our Heavenly Father to Mother Eugenia Ravasio (in a Church approved private revelation):

"Tell them that they have a Father who, having created them, wants to give them the treasures He possesses. Above all, tell them that I think of them, I love them and want to give them eternal happiness….Tell them to come to Me: I will help them, I will lighten their burden and sweeten their hard life. I will inebriate them with My fatherly love, to make them happy in time and eternity."[27]

"To recite the Rosary is nothing other than to *contemplate with Mary the face of Christ*" (St. John Paul II).

Endnotes

1. Saint John Paul II. *Crossing the Threshold of Hope,* pg. 228. New York: Alfred A. Knopf, Inc., 1994.

2. For history of the Scapular of Our Lady of Mount Carmel see: www.sistersofcarmel.com/brown-scapular-information.php.

3. For history of the discovery of the relics of St. Anne, read: *Good St. Anne.* Tan Books and Publishers, Inc., 1999.

4. St. Louis de Montfort. *The Secret of the Rosary,* 18.

5. Saint John Paul II. *The Rosary of the Virgin Mary,* 30.

6. Saint John Paul II. *The Rosary of the Virgin Mary,* 25.

7. Gallagher, Timothy M. *The Examen Prayer, pg. 25*

8. Our Lady of Fatima, May 13, 1917. www.dailycatholic.org/issue/2000May/may9fat.htm

9. Saint John Paul II. *Crossing the Threshold of Hope,* pg. 228.

10. Saint John Paul II. *The Rosary of the Virgin Mary*, 35.

11. Saint John Paul II. *The Rosary of the Virgin Mary*, 1.

12. Saint John Paul II. *The Rosary of the Virgin Mary*, 4.

13. Saint John Paul II. *The Rosary of the Virgin Mary*, 2.

14. Saint John Paul II. *The Rosary of the Virgin Mary*, 37.

15. Saint John Paul II. *The Rosary of the Virgin Mary*, 19.

16. *Catechism of the Catholic Church*, 1213

17. Pope Benedict XVI. *Jesus of Nazareth*. pp. 251-252

18. Saint John Paul II. *The Rosary of the Virgin Mary*, 9, 21.

19. Saint John Paul II. *Man and Woman He Created Them,* 93.

20. www.buffalonews.com/city/article214083.ece

21. Saint John Paul II. *The Rosary of the Virgin Mary*, 13.

22. Saint John Paul II. *The Rosary of the Virgin Mary*, 23.

23. Saint John Paul II. *The Rosary of the Virgin Mary*, 23.

24. Saint John Paul II. *The Rosary of the Virgin Mary*, 8.

25. Saint John Paul II. *The Rosary of the Virgin Mary*, 24.

26. Audrey Keenan. E-mail to Sister Mary Rose on September 4, 2013.

27. Sister Eugenia Elisabetta Ravasio. *The Father Speaks to His Children.*

Bibliography

Saint John Paul II. *Crossing the Threshold of Hope*. New York: Alfred A. Knopf, Inc., 1994.

Saint John Paul II. *Man and Woman He Created Them-- A Theology of the Body*. Boston: Pauline Books and Media, 2006.

Saint John Paul II. *The Rosary of the Virgin Mary*. Boston: Pauline Books and Media, 2002.

Catechism of the Catholic Church. Second Edition. Citta del Vaticano: Libreria Editrice Vaticano, 1994.

Dombroski, Sister Mary Agnes. *Interactive on-line Rosary*. www.stcharleshome.org/rosary

Gallagher, Timothy M. *The Examen Prayer*. New York: The Crossroad Publishing Company, 2006.

Holy Bible (Translation is from the Confraternity of Christian Doctrine — a Revision of the Challoner-Rheims Version Copyright 1984, 1955 by the Daughters of St. Paul).

Pope Benedict XVI. *Jesus of Nazareth*. Doubleday, 2007.

Sister Eugenia Elisabetta Ravasio. *The Father Speaks to His Children*. L'Aquila, Italy: "Pater" Publications, 1989.

St. Louis de Montfort. *The Secret of the Rosary*. Bay Shore, NY: Montfort Publications, 1969.

St. Louis de Montfort. *True Devotion to Mary*. Rockford, IL: Tan Books, 1985.

West, Christopher. *Heaven's Song; Sexual Love as it was Meant to Be*. West Chester, PA: Ascension Press, 2008.

Photography credits:

Most of the pictures used to illustrate the Mysteries were taken at St. Charles Children's Home in Rochester, NH by Mother Paul Marie or Sister Mary Rose. Larry Landolfi took the pictures for the Wedding Feast at Cana and The Crowning With Thorns. The picture of the Birth of Christ is from the nativity crèche at Our Lady of the Holy Rosary parish in Rochester, NH. The figures in this crèche were hand carved by Louis Sarvary (d. 2003). The picture for the Agony of the Garden is also from Our Lady of the Holy Rosary parish in Rochester, NH. The pictures of Bishop Libasci signing the recommendation and the picture illustrating the Institution of the Eucharist (photographed in the Most Merciful Heart of Jesus Perpetual Adoration Chapel in Our Lady of the Holy Rosary Church) were taken by Jennifer Gilbert. The Rosary drawing is courtesy of St. Vincent Pallotti Catholic Church Religious Education; Abilene, TX. The picture of Adam Keenan is from the Keenan family. The L.A.S.T. picture was taken by Meg Wood.

Fifteen Promises of the Rosary

Our Blessed Mother, during the thirteenth century made fifteen promises to St. Dominic and Blessed Alan de la Roche for those who pray the Rosary faithfully:

1. Whosoever shall faithfully serve me by the recitation of the Rosary shall receive signal graces.

2. I promise my special protection and the greatest graces to all those who shall recite the Rosary.

3. The Rosary shall be a powerful armor against hell, it will destroy vice, decrease sin and defeat heresies.

4. It will cause good works to flourish; it will obtain for souls the abundant mercy of God; it will withdraw the hearts of men from the love of the world and its vanities, and will lift them to the desire for Eternal Things. Oh, that souls would sanctify themselves by this means.

5. The soul which recommends itself to me by the recitation of the Rosary shall not perish.

6. Whosoever shall recite the Rosary devoutly, applying himself to the consideration of its Sacred Mysteries shall never be conquered by misfortune. God will not chastise him in His justice, he shall not perish by an un-provided death; if he be just he shall remain in the grace of God, and become worthy of Eternal Life.

7. Whoever shall have a true devotion for the Rosary shall not die without the Sacraments of the Church.

8. Those who are faithful to recite the Rosary shall have during their life and at their death the Light of God and the plenitude of His Graces; at the moment of death they shall participate in the Merits of the Saints in Paradise.

9. I shall deliver from purgatory those who have been devoted to the Rosary.

10. The faithful children of the Rosary shall merit a high degree of Glory in Heaven.

11. You shall obtain all you ask of me by recitation of the Rosary.

12. All those who propagate the Holy Rosary shall be aided by me in their necessities.

13. I have obtained from my Divine Son that all the advocates of the Rosary shall have for intercessors the entire Celestial Court during their life and at the hour of death.

14. All who recite the Rosary are my Sons, and brothers of my Only Son Jesus Christ.

15. Devotion to my Rosary is a great sign of predestination.[1]

---

[1] http://www.ourladyswarriors.org/prayer/15promise.htm

List of the Mysteries of the Rosary:

Joyful:

1. The Annunciation
2. The Visitation
3. The Birth of Jesus
4. The Presentation of Jesus in the Temple
5. The Finding of Jesus in the Temple

Luminous:

1. The Baptism of Jesus
2. The Wedding Feast at Cana
3. The Proclamation of the Kingdom of God
4. The Transfiguration
5. The Institution of the Eucharist

Sorrowful:

1. The Agony in the Garden
2. The Scourging at the Pillar
3. The Crowning with Thorns
4. The Carrying of the Cross
5. The Crucifixion

Glorious:

1. The Resurrection
2. The Ascension
3. The Descent of the Holy Spirit
4. The Assumption
5. The Crowning of the Blessed Virgin Mary as Queen of Heaven and Earth

About the Author's Religious Community:

Sister Mary Rose Reddy is a member of the **Daughters of Mary, Mother of Healing Love (www.motherofhealinglove.org).** The Sisters' focus is the healing of families through devotion to Jesus through Mary and various forms of teaching and catechesis. One of their prayer initiatives is the **Lifeline Against Suicide Team (L.A.S.T.)**.

"Do thyself no harm, for we are all here" (Acts 16:28).

Lifeline Against Suicide Team (L.A.S.T.) Prayer

Heavenly Father, we thank You for the gift of every human life. In the Name of Jesus we ask You to send Your Holy Spirit to each and every person from the beginning to the end of time that all may appreciate the gift of life.

We pray for all who are tempted to commit suicide that Your Spirit would convince them that they are beautiful, irreplaceable, and greatly loved.

We pray for all those who have committed suicide that Jesus, Who is outside of time, will open the fullness of His Merciful Loving Heart to each of them as they realize the terrible mistake which they have made.

We pray for all families and friends who are grieving suicides. Heavenly Father, please take all their prayers, tears, grief, love, and regrets and unite them to Your Son's sacrificial death on the Cross. May this united Sacrifice, along with the prayers and tears of Our Mother of Sorrows, and all the Holy Angels and Saints, bring Your abundant Life to those who have died by suicide and to the people of every time and place.

We ask this in the Name of Jesus Christ, Your Son Who lives and reigns with You and the Holy Spirit, One God forever and ever. Amen.

Approved by Most Rev. Peter A. Libasci, Bishop of Manchester: 10-2-2014

"O Key of David, Opening the Gates of God's Eternal Kingdom: Come and free the Prisoners of darkness."

(from the Gospel Antiphon December 20th)

To purchase more copies of this book or find out more about the Daughters of Mary, Mother of Healing Love please go to: http://motherofhealinglove.org/book/